Six-Pack Abs in 60 Days

The Easy Way to a New, Slimmer Midsection

Six-Pack Abs in 60 Days

Published by MuscleMag International
5775 McLaughlin Road
Mississauga, ON
Canada L5R 3P7

Designed by Jackie Kydyk
Edited by Mandy Morgan

10 9 8 7 6 5 4 3 2 Pbk.

Canadian Cataloguing in Publication Data

Kennedy, Robert, 1938-
    Six-pack abs in sixty days: the easy way to a slimmer midsection

Includes bibliographical references and index.
ISBN 1-55210-011-1

    1. Exercise. 2. Abdomen--Muscles. I. Hines, Dwayne, 1961-
II.Title.

RA781.6.K45 1998   646.7'5   C98-900851-7

Distributed in Canada by
CANBOOK Distribution Services
1220 Nicholson Road
Newmarket, ON
L3Y 7V1
800-399-6858

Distributed in the States by
BookWorld Services
1933 Whitfield Park Loop
Sarasota, FL 34243
800-444-2524

Printed in Canada

This book is dedicated to Janet and to the trainers who made me work on my abdominals: My father, Coach Reyes, Coach Campbell, Coach Hudson, Coach Trent, Coach Russell, Dr. Ollie McClay, Sgt. Tyson, Sgt. Swift, and Gordon Oster.

Table of Contents

Chapter One

Chapter Two

Chapter Three

Chapter Four

Chapter Five

Women concur that one of the most noticeable regions of a man's physique is his waist.

CHAPTER ONE
The Comprehensive Approach

What is the most amazing muscle group? The biceps? The chest? Everyone and his dog has an opinion. So why not consult an expert on the physique – someone like Arnold Schwarzenegger? Arnold is known for having one of the greatest physiques of all time. Arnold noted that the abdominals are the best muscle group when he wrote, "I think a beautifully developed midsection is the most immediately impressive part of the male physique. If you are familiar with Greek mythology or classical sculpture you have no doubt seen the photographs of the various gods and how each had fantastic abdominal muscles. Well-sculptured, highly defined abdominals give the physique a more finished appearance than any other muscle group."[1] He is not the only person to hold such an opinion about the midsection. The late Vince Gironda noted that "sharp, well-built abdominal muscles are worth a king's ransom. To my mind, there is no more treasured possession."[2] Men often think that it is their muscular arms or massive chest that catches a lady's eye, but most ladies concur that one of the most noticeable regions of a man's physique is the waist.

Arnold Schwarzenegger

Arnold, Vince, and the ladies are all correct. The waistline is the key area for developing the "look" of the body. Certainly each muscle group contributes to the entire look, but the abdominals contribute the most. If any other muscle group is underpar you might notice it in an offhand manner, but if the waistline is bloated, it really stands out. Think about this – a physique that has been developed to a high degree with massive muscular arms, a big chest, strong legs . . . and a fat, bulging waist. The oversized midsection detracts from the rest of the body. In fact, it becomes the focus of every-one's attention. No matter how well you develop the rest of your body, you cannot afford to neglect the waist. Try as you might to ignore it – a fat waistline is gross – there is no way around it.

THE V-SHAPE

One of the classical elements of a good-looking body is the V-shape, formed by a wide upper torso (chest, shoulders and back) tapering down to a small waist-line. This striking look is ruined however, if you have a large waist. Do you want all of the hard work put into building a dynamic upper body to be overshadowed by a fat waistline? Of course not. Obtaining the V-shape is essential and crucial to have that "hot" physique that turns heads. You won't be able to come anywhere near acquiring this look if you don't get a handle on your abdominals.

No matter how well you develop the rest of your body, you cannot afford to neglect your waist.

Art Dilkes

SCULPTING A SUPER STOMACH

Arnold mentioned the concept of "sculpting" the abdominals. This is an excellent and very descriptive expression of the correct type of training that will conquer the waist. The waist is an area that should be perfected in the same manner as a sculptor creates something definite out of an undefined mass. And that is what a lot of people have around their midsection – undefined mass. Or perhaps worse – mass defined as fat. But there is hope. The abdominals respond rapidly to training. The late Vince Gironda noted that "the abdominals develop easily."[3] But that does not mean the training is not tough. In the initial stages, especially if you have not trained the abdominals for some time or at all, you will experience quite

Hamdullah Aykutlu

a bit of pain. But as you continue to train, your body and mind will adapt to the pain and you will progress. The workouts outlined in the Six-Pack Abs program will work particularly well as they employ gradual and incremental principles, which means you work up to more challenging workouts as you progress through the program. The idea is to gradually increase the work on the abdominals until they are suffi-ciently challenged to respond in a muscular manner. However, this does not mean tons and tons of exercises or sets of exercises. The stomach works better with an average number of sets. Vince Gironda wrote that "the abdominals do not have to be worked with dozens of sets of high repetitions every day . . . you will smooth out your abs and subject your system to a degree of shock that can hinder gains if you overwork these sensitive muscles."[4] Arnold Schwarzenegger also points out the problem of over-training. "Training too much is as bad – if not worse – than not training enough. Somehow you will have to trust your body to tell you when you are overtraining. It lets you know through excessive aches and pains."[5] Notice that Arnold states one should be wary of "excessive pain"; however, that doesn't mean there is no pain involved in training. After all, Arnold made popular the statement "no pain, no gain." There is quite a bit of pain involved if one is to expect improvement. Training the body literally involves changing the physique. This doesn't happen lightly. Change in the body comes about through a toughly contested bout with the body. You can't get an awesome waist by sitting on the sofa eating cupcakes and pizza. All good things cost, and the higher the value, the higher the payment. So expect some challenge in the Six-Pack Abs training program.

TRIM AND TIGHT

One of the major reasons why training the abdominals is so important is because a tight waist is the prime indicator of a trim and tight physique and excellent fitness conditioning. A trim and tight physique is a major commodity in today's world. In fact, it has always been a valuable asset. Arnold mentioned the Greek sculptures and the focus placed on their waists. Since ancient times, a trim, tight, and muscular physique has stood out as ideal. To this day the most ideal physique is the one with six-pack abs. Most people don't realize this fact, don't have the knowledge, or are not disciplined enough to change their waist area. The Six-Pack Abs course will provide you with the facts and training program to put you in the rare minority who have a trim and tight midsection.

A trim and tight waistline also has many other benefits – health, protection and attractiveness.

COMPREHENSIVE CONCEPT

The major concept to be mastered when it comes to the waist-training approach is that your training must be comprehensive in nature. That is, you cannot get maximum or even consistent gains by neglecting any of the three major pillars of midsection mastery, as they combine to produce a synergistic effect determining the shape and muscularity of the midsection. These areas attack the abdominals together, forcing the change that is necessary for maximum development. The three areas are like the legs of a three-legged stool – if any of the three are missing, the stool tips over. The same is true for training the waist – you need to hit all three areas hard and consistently to receive all of the results your body is capable of producing. The "triple training attack" is the best way to build the body's midsection into awesome proportions. Some people make the mistake of working on just one area and expecting to see amazing results. Unless you are amazingly gifted in the genetic arena, you cannot make major changes through the use of only one of the areas. What are the areas? The "triple training attack" consists of direct abdominal work, diet, and aerobic exercise. The Six-Pack Abs program utilizes all three areas as the most comprehensive, effective, and efficient manner in which to work the waist. As noted earlier, some people make the mistake of picking one area and going all out to "whip the waist into shape." They may do 500 or more situps a day and instantly expect a super stomach. Or they may cut their caloric intake in half and expect a midsection miracle. Others take up a

Milos Sarcev

running, jogging, or swimming program and think it alone will totally take care of their waist. And to some degree each area will produce some effect. But none of these areas individually hold a candle to the synergistic effect brought on by the "triple training attack." Focusing on only one of the three areas is a mistake. For instance, one young man had an oversized midsection and decided to do something about the problem. He thought that 1000 situps a day would cure the problem. So he began to perform 1000 situps daily, however, he continued to eat as much or more than he had ever eaten, and he didn't engage in any cardio-vascular work. (His situps were performed in 50 to 100 repetition groups so that he did not receive any fat-burning benefits from the situps.) Soon he became discouraged and his daily situp count began to drop. Disappointed with the lack of progress, he quit altogether, which was particularly embarrassing since he had made a great deal out of his "waist reduction program." His story is repeated by many other people each year. They get all excited and fired-up about taking control of their waistline and start doing hundreds of situps or some other waist exercise and then quit when they find their stomach does not have the incredible "jewel" appearance as seen in the fitness magazines. The same thing is often true with those who use a diet to attempt to control the shape of their stomach. They force themselves to cut out most of the "junk" food and drastically lower their caloric intake. They do notice some benefit, but usually quit after failing to find any trace of the famed "washboard" appearance they were so hoping for. (Failed diets are one of the most frequent occurrences known to mankind.) The

No pain, no gain.

Flex Wheeler, Paul Dillet and Kevin Levrone

third area of midsection-training also has similar pitfalls. Many people decide to go gung-ho on some aerobic workout (such as jogging) on the power of a New Year's resolution only to give up the endeavor after several weeks without noticing any real stomach muscularity. Their reliance on one tool to totally reshape their midsection is a mistake.

What would change these scenarios is understanding that waist-training is not a one-factor effort. The "triple attack," which creates a synergistic effect, is the ultimate manner in which to master the midsection. To get the best results and to obtain continuous results, it is essential to grasp the concept that you must focus on three areas. Again, these areas are direct abdominal work, diet, and aerobic fitness. Each area has a beneficial effect, contributing significantly to sculpting a super stomach; however there are also pitfalls to each area. For instance, the old-fashion situp is not the most effective way to perform direct abdominal work. And diet alone will do essentially nothing to help you achieve a muscular midsection. It is important to know the strengths and weaknesses of each of the three areas of waist-training. The following chapters of the Six-Pack Abs program contain an in-depth look at each of these areas and how they can be utilized to give you the Six-Pack Abs you desire. If you did not realize how important the concept of comprehensive training is for the waist, hopefully you do now. Check out the following chapters for "news you can use" and put that knowledge to use.

Lee Apperson

THE MIGHTY MIND

The mind plays just as big a part as the body in any successful training program. Your mind is what will make or break your success in building awesome abdominals. Vince Gironda noted that "the mind's power is awesome!"[6] especially in reference to the mind and body connection in fitness. Arnold Schwarzenegger also points to the power of the mind over the body.[7] Your mind, not your body, will determine whether or not you succeed at sculpting your waist into the tight and trim muscle group that you want it to be. Use your mind to block out the negative thoughts and replace them with positive thoughts and actions. You can drastically change your waist. It is possible, you too can have six-pack abs.

A SUPER STOMACH IN 60 DAYS?

Can you obtain a super stomach in just 60 days? Training the waist is an ongoing process – even those with the best physiques have to maintain their body by working out on a consistent basis. But they do reach a "maintenance"

Mohamad Makkawy

stage where their workouts are much easier than when they were beginners. To attain and keep a "hot" waistline you have to use the three pillars (direct abdominal workouts, diet, and aerobic exercise) on a regular and consistent basis. The good news is that some of your quickest gains will most likely occur in the initial stages of your training program – in the first two months. However, the body adapts and will give a smaller return for your effort as you progress in your training – the principle of diminishing returns. The most drastic changes generally occur in the initial stages. This is more true for the waist than any other area. Vince Gironda said that he developed world-class abdominals in just six weeks![8] As mentioned earlier, the waist responds rapidly to training. Of course, if you have an excessive amount of fat around the waist then of course it will take some time to diet down and burn it off with aerobic work. The more fat you have, the longer it will take. But the essential groundwork will be set down in the first couple of months if you work hard at it. The Six-Pack Abs course will help you make the most rapid transition from where you are to where you want to be. The combination of elements used in the comprehensive abdominal-training approach is the best possible way to make your midsection "hot" in a hurry. Read through the material, take notes, try out the workouts, add or delete items according to your specific needs, put in some real effort, and watch as your abdominals take form.

> **Your mind is what will make or break your success in building awesome abdominals.**

References

1. Arnold Schwarzenegger and Douglas Kent Hall, Arnold: The Education of a Bodybuilder (New York: Wallaby Pocket Books, 1977), 206.
2. Vince Gironda and Robert Kennedy, Unleashing the Wild Physique (New York: Sterling Publishing, 1984), 107.
3. Gironda, Wild Physique, 105.
4. Gironda, Wild Physique, 106.
5. Schwarzenegger, Education of a Bodybuilder, 192.
6. Gironda, Wild Physique, 76.
7. Schwarzenegger, Education of a Bodybuilder, 88.
8. Gironda, Wild Physique, 105.

Bill Davey and Brandy Hale

CHAPTER TWO

The Waist Workouts

The first of the three primary elements of sculpting six-pack abs is the waist workout. The waist workouts are designed to do one thing – add muscularity to the midsection. The waist workouts are not designed to burn off calories and reduce fat from the physique. If some small fat reduction and caloric loss occurs, great, but the primary and sole emphasis of the waist workouts is to progressively challenge the muscles located in the abdominal region. Fat loss will come from the other two areas, diet and aerobic work, so the focus of the waist workouts is on the muscles. Do not try to make the waist workout a fat-burning session unless you have inordinate amounts of time to waste on your midsection. Keep your concentration on the muscles.

THE PAIN FACTOR

One inescapable fact of life in training the abdominals is the pain factor. Waist-training is not easy. It hurts to continue to perform repetition after repetition on the waist muscles. However, it is crucial to fight through the pain barrier. The pain barrier is that point in the workout where the pain in the muscle region becomes so intense that you feel you cannot go on. But the best training comes at and beyond this point. If you always stop short of muscle failure you will not realize your full potential. The pain barrier occurs at different points for different people, so only you can push yourself to the outer limits of the pain barrier. Your pain barrier should shift as you become accustomed to working on your abdominals. You will be able to endure more and get a higher repetition count on each exercise.

If you want to look tough, you have to train tough. You won't get sharp, accurately defined abdominals unless you work at it – hard. It was mentioned that many people can get

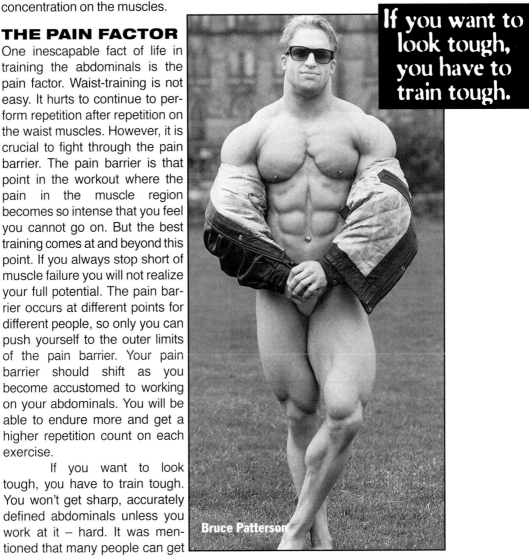

If you want to look tough, you have to train tough.

Bruce Patterson

"hot" abdominals fairly quickly. But quickly does not necessarily mean easily. The Six-Pack Abs routine calls for some beastly workouts on your part. However, remember, it is best to work up to the tougher stuff. Don't try to become a brute in one night.

SETS AND REPETITIONS

A repetition is one single movement, from start to finish, of any exercise. A repetition of a situp would be moving from the flat position to an upper position and then back down to the flat position again. A set is a group of repetitions performed nonstop. Several sets are performed for each exercise. Sets and repetitions enable you to focus on one exercise at a time for maximum concentration and productivity.

INCREMENTAL TRAINING

Abdominal-training, as all other training, should be performed in an incremental manner. This means that you gradually increase the challenge to your muscles as they adapt to the initial training. Your body will grudgingly adapt to the difficulty of the workout by building the muscles up to a point where they can handle the workout. This takes some time, but your abdominals will become stronger and able to handle more. It is important not to stop at this point. Stopping at any level shifts your training from moving ahead into maintenance gear. Maintenance is fine if you want to stay where you are, but not if you want to progress. To move ahead you must increase the difficulty of the training routine.

Flex Wheeler

Don't try to become a brute in one night.

Progressing from the simple to the more complex (or difficult) routine is the best training approach possible. Learn the basics, and let your body get used to the physical challenge. Your body gradually adjusts so that you can handle the harder stuff, and you also protect yourself from injury. It is not wise to try to conquer your waist in a single week – at best you will end up sore, and worse, may injure yourself. Most likely you will quit. A gradual ascension to the more difficult levels of training is the best path to success. The Six Pack Abs training program provides guidance on just how to do that.

Nasser El Sonbaty

The increments that will be used as the controlling factors for the workout are the amount of exercises, sets, and repetitions. In weight training the amount of weight used is one of the controlling factors, but not for waist training.

WEIGHTLESS WAIST-TRAINING

Weight training is the best manner in which to train the human body – but not the midsection. Virtually every other area of the body is best built through weight training; however, the waist region is a different story. It is better to use little or no weights when training the waist for a very specific reason. When any muscle is trained with progressive resistance it grows larger. The waist is no exception. You can get bulky waist muscles that will protrude too far and obscure the lines of the waist. This is not the look you're after. The best waist is narrow and muscular – tight and trim. This look is spoiled by an over-bulked waist, whether that bulk comes from muscle or fat. You can avoid the excess size by not using the heavy weights that some people do. Perform most of your waist work in a "bodyweight only" mode. It is alright to occasionally use weight when waist-training, but not good as a steady habit if you want to keep that region trim. The same holds true for side bends. Side bends with dumbells build up the obliques, but that is the last place in the world where you want to put on size. A wide pair of obliques destroys the V-shape that most people are striving to attain. The exercises in the Six-Pack Abs routine are performed without weights, and in fairly high-repetition ranges.

WORKOUT FREQUENCY

How often should you work on your waist? A better question is, "How quickly do you want to see awesome results?" Most muscle groups need about 48 hours to regroup. It is standard training procedure to take at least a day or two off for each bodypart that is trained. This is not necessarily true for the waist. The midsection is a tough muscle group and can be worked every day. The best scenario is to work the waist 4 to 6 times a week, allowing only a couple of days rest for the abdominals. However, if you find that you are having a difficult time recovering from your midsection-training, take one day off between waist workouts. This will allow you to get in at least three or four workouts per week.

Hamdullah Aykutlu

WORK OUT ANYWHERE, ANYTIME

One of the benefits of working your waist is that you don't need any equipment to do the job. When you use weights you need a certain amount of equipment or a membership at a local club; however, this is not necessary for midsection muscularity. You can train anywhere you have a little space. Your workouts don't have to come to an end when you are traveling either. The waist workout has the most minimal requirements of any exercise. There are other benefits also. You won't need a ton of money to work on your waist. In fact, you can get in a great abdominal workout without spending a penny because you do not need to join an expensive gym or buy some fancy chrome gadgets. The best exercises for the waist are basic and performed freehand. So don't let the excuse of lack of money or opportunity keep you from a fantastic waist.

The time element is another positive factor. Since you don't necessarily need to travel to a gym (you can work out in your room or backyard) you have extra time to spend on midsection-training. A good waist workout does not need to take much time. The best waist workouts are tough and brief. So time and money (or rather, lack of) shouldn't stop you from shaping a super stomach.

TOP GUNS

There are three exercises that are probably more famous than any of the other exercises combined. These are the pushup, the chinup, and the situp. These three exercises were the "only game in town" for several decades. Their popularity was spread through their use by the military and sports coaches. Recently, weight training has started to slip past these three as a more popular and productive way to exercise the muscles, but the pushup, chinup, and situp will most likely always be used by someone, somewhere. What does this have to do with your waist? One of these three exercises, the situp, has been the most popular manner in which to work the waist for thousands and thousands of people. But, unfortunately, the situp is not the best exercise for the waist.

SITUPS

The situp movement does not work the midsection as directly as do many other excellent waist-training exercises. As Vince Gironda put it, "Most people are unaware that the full situp and leg-raise exercises are not primarily abdominal movements. True, there is some midsection involvement, but they are not pure waistline exercises. Few understand that the action of the abdominal muscles is to shorten the distance between the pelvic basin and the sternum. It has little to do with full leg raises or situps, except in the contracted range of the movement when the distance is shortened between the pelvis and sternum. The partial situp is a better abdominal builder."[1] The situp does have some benefit, but not as much as it is thought to. It works on other muscles besides the waist – including the upper legs. The situp works the psoas muscle, the muscle attached to the upper thighbones, which functions by pulling the body to a sitting position.[2] For the best abdominal work, the situp is not the number one exercise. This may be difficult to accept for some people since they have been using the situp as the mainstay of their workout program for so long. But why waste time on an average waist exercise when you could use an excellent waist exercise and see better results in a shorter period of time? Sure, you have seen some people with great abdominals who have performed situps, but perhaps their waist would have

To move ahead you must increase the difficulty of the training routine.

Mike Matarazzo, Paul Dillett and J.J. Marsh

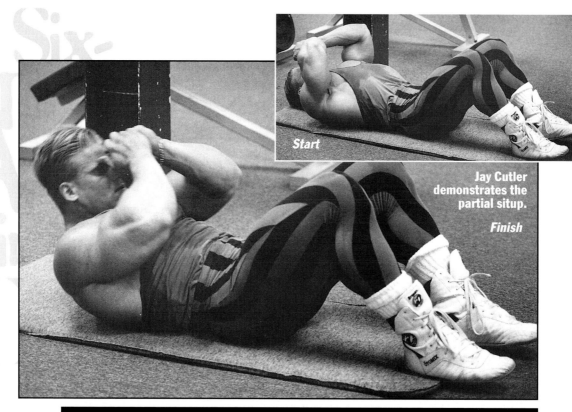

Start

Jay Cutler demonstrates the partial situp.

Finish

Try to add a few repetitions each workout.

looked even better if they used a superior exercise. Besides, some people are genetically gifted, and would get great abdominals if they just jumped around on one foot. The best abdominal exercises are those that focus on working the narrowly defined area that the abdominals lie in. These exercises that put the spotlight on the stomach are going to be featured next. The exercises will be described in detail, and then a progressive program putting the exercises to work will follow.

PARTIAL SITUPS

As Vince Gironda mentioned, the partial situp is a much better movement for training the midsection. The partial situp is sometimes called the "half situp" and is actually much more difficult to do than the regular situp because the feet are not braced in this movement. The partial situp is performed from the starting position of the normal situp. Bend the knees and bring the body up between 1/4 to 1/2 the distance of the regular situp, where the back just barely leaves the ground on the upswing. For the best results, don't tuck your hands behind your head – hold them in front of your torso. After a few repetitions this exercise should become difficult to perform, however, continue to push yourself as far as possible. Don't cheat! Keep working at this exercise until you can master it. A good goal to work up to is 100 of these partial situps in a nonstop fashion. But don't be discouraged if you cannot come near that number at first. It takes time, effort, and patience to achieve a highly developed waist. Remember the incremental factor mentioned earlier. Gradually work your way up to a higher repetition range. Try to add a few repetitions each workout. Perhaps 100 repetitions is no problem for you. If so, shoot for 200. The goal is to challenge your body (however it is genetically configured), not someone else's body. So base the challenge of how many repetitions you can handle on your specific goals.

CRUNCHES

The situp was the top waist exercise for a long time, but it has been dethroned. The new king is the crunch. The crunch is a waist exercise that works the waist much more directly than the situp does. Many people are switching to the crunch once they experience the benefits of this unique exercise. The most effective stomach movement is one which enables the abdominal muscles to shorten the distance between the pelvic basin and the sternum.[3] The crunch does exactly that. The crunch is performed with the back flat against the floor. Slowly raise the head, neck, shoulders and arms as a unit (with hands resting gently behind the ears) as the knees are raised at the same time (lower legs parallel to the floor). Touch the elbows to the knee/thigh area (or come as close as you possibly can). Hold for a second or two, then lower to the original position. For the best results, don't allow your head or feet to rest on the floor in the down position, keep them slightly off the ground to maintain tension on the waist. Repeat the action. As you bring the elbows into the knee/thigh area, exhale fully. For an even more intense workout, hold the upper position for five seconds. Several sets of this exercise will work wonders for your waist. Use the crunch as a primary abdominal exercise in your training arsenal. If you are limited by time and can only perform a couple of waist exercises, make certain you include the crunch.

"BICYCLE" CRUNCHES

Another excellent abdominal exercise is the "bicycle" crunch. This exercise is a variation of the regular crunch and gives the waist an even fuller workout than the regular crunch. Start the exercise in the same position as the crunch (face up, hands behind your ears). Pull the elbows up as the knees come up in a slow manner, rotating one elbow to touch the opposite knee. For example, if you rotated the right elbow, you would tap it on the left knee. Lower your body (but not all the way), then come back up again, this time touching the opposite elbow to the opposite knee (the one that was not touched in the last move). Each full movement (a rotation to both the left and right knees with opposite elbows) counts as one repetition. The "bicycle" crunch works the abdominals from all angles (the twisting motion really gives the side abdominals a good burn), making it a superior exercise.

The "bicycle" crunch works the abdominals from all angles. – Bob Paris

Start

Finish

EXTENDED CRUNCHES

The next exercise for the waist is the extended crunch. The extended crunch is simply the crunch movement performed in an exaggerated position. Instead of holding the feet in the air, place them on an elevated platform such as a bench, stool, or chair. Make certain that the platform is stable and able to hold your lower body. Perform the extended crunch movement pushing your thighs upward and inward as your head and elbows come toward the thigh area. This upward movement puts more stress on the waist muscles and develops them quickly. For an extra tough challenge, try holding your body in the upward position for a couple of seconds before returning to the ground. As with the other exercises, exhale as you rise and inhale as you return to the starting position.

Rich Gaspari develops his abdominals with extended crunches.

Finish

Start

SIDE CRUNCHES

The side crunch is another variation of the regular crunch. However, instead of working the center muscles of the abdominals, this exercise works the side abdominals, the obliques. Some action from the middle abdominals is also included. Lie flat on your back, hands behind your head as with the other crunch movements. Place your legs in a down and out position (this position looks somewhat like a splayed frog). Instead of pulling your head upward, pull the elbow on one side (with both hands clasped behind the head) toward the knee on the same side of the body. At the same time, pull the knee toward the elbow. Keep your body touching the floor throughout the exercise. Simply tip to one side, then the other. You will need a bit more room to perform this exercise than with the other waist exercises since you will be "gyrating" back and forth in a supine circular motion. This exercise may be a little funny looking, but it is very effective for the obliques, a necessary area to train if you want your waist to look complete and awesome from every angle. Tight and trim obliques look especially fantastic.

Mohamad Makkawy

SIDE BENDS

The side bend is another exercise that works the obliques. As mentioned earlier, the obliques should never be trained with weights! You want to define the waist, not thicken it. Weight-trained obliques get bigger, and if you have some fat in that area, your entire side will look rather large – and quite unattractive. Use a high-repetition count instead of weights. With your feet more than shoulder width apart, bend down and touch your hand to the side of the knee area, then switch to the other side. Keep your back as flat as possible during the exercise.

V-RAISES

The V-raise is an excellent exercise for the lower abdominals as they can be hard to isolate. The upper abdominal area is much easier to stimulate through stomach exercises, but you can dynamize the lower area if you use the right exercises. The V-raise is one such exercise. Lie flat on the floor, face up. Raise your hands above your head as high as possible. Slowly raise both the hands and feet, bringing them together above your stomach area. During this exercise your body will form a "V" shape as you raise your extremities. One way to perfect your technique is to visualize your stomach region as a hinge. The body moves from both ends as the stomach stays stationary. The lower abdominals will get a great workout with this exercise.

Tight and trim obliques look especially fantastic.

LEG RAISES

The leg raise is another exceptional exercise. The leg raise is an exercise used by a lot of sports coaches. It concentrates most of the effort on the lower abdominal region. To perform this exercise, lie on your back with your legs extended straight out in front of you. Place your hands under the sides of your buttocks. Slowly raise your feet until they are eight to 10 inches off the ground. Hold this position for four to five seconds, then touch your feet to the ground and repeat. For variation, raise one leg over the other, switching on the following repetition. This exercise is tough and will help build your stamina in addition to your lower midsection.

LEG ROLLS

This unique maneuver trains the lower abdominals. Lie on your back on a raised object (a wide bench or the corner of a bed works great). Place your hands by the sides of your buttocks. Cross your feet but open your legs, keeping your knees bent. Your buttocks should be on the edge of the bench, bed, or whatever object you are laying on. Roll your hips down, then bring them up, pulling the knees up toward your stationary arms. Keep the motion slow and smooth. You will really feel this through the entire midsection, especially the lower region.

LEG-RAISE CRUNCHES

The leg-raise crunch is an exercise that works the full abdominal muscle group. It is a tough exercise because it gives the waist no time for rest. To perform this awesome abdominal movement, start from a position flat on your back. Place your hands behind your head and perform a crunch, at the same time raising your legs (kept straight up to a level where they are just above your waist. Lower your head as you simultaneously lower your legs; however, do not let your feet touch the ground. Instead, put them in the position of the regular leg raise (eight to 10 inches off the ground), then raise them again as you pull your upper body forward in the crunch motion. This constant stress on the midsection is brutal, but it delivers results! Both your upper and lower abdominal muscles will wonder what hit them after this nasty exercise. Move slowly throughout the movement maintaining control (as much as possible!) at all times. This is a difficult, yet effective exercise so make it part of your routine.

Jamo Nezzar

TUMMY TUCKS

One of the best ways to handle your waist is to practice the tummy-tuck exercise. Simply suck your waist in, and hold it in as far as possible for as long as possible. You can do this exercise in the car, at work, wherever. The more you perform the tummy tuck, the better. It is said that if you always practice keeping your stomach in tight, it will soon become a full-time habit. And this exercise is a good habit to have. At first it will feel somewhat exaggerated to hold your stomach in, but soon the muscles will adjust and it will begin to feel normal. You can add to your appearance right away by performing tummy-tuck exercises throughout the day.

HANGING LEG RAISES

The hanging leg raise works the full abdominals. You can also work the intercostals, muscles that run alongside the abdominals, with a slight variation of the hanging leg raise. The intercostals are worked by lifting your knees from side to side (alternately) in a slow and controlled manner. It is good to work both types of this exercise into your routine, performing a couple of sets of knee raises to the front, and a couple of sets with knee raises to the sides. For a tougher workout on the front raises, keep your legs straight as you lift them, instead of bent.

ABDOMINAL VACUUMS

Vince Gironda was famous for promoting several unique exercises. One of these is the abdominal vacuum. The abdominal vacuum is an exercise that can be performed several times throughout the day. The exercise is performed by bending forward and putting your hands on a table, chair, countertop, or bench. Bend the knees slightly and hunch the back to remove pressure from the lower body, allowing the focus to be on the waist. Pull your stomach muscles in as far and as hard as possible. Hold this position for two to five seconds, then totally relax the waist. Repeat for several repetitions. Like the tummy tuck, continual use of this exercise will form the habit of having the waist muscles drawn in tight at all times. Take advantage of any opportunity you have during the day to pop out a few repetitions of the abdominal vacuum.

Start

Lee Apperson demonstrates hanging leg raises.

Finish

For a tougher workout keep your legs straight during hanging leg raises instead of bent.

POSTURE

Your posture also has a bearing upon the abdominal region. Your posture, whether sitting or standing, is contributing to the way your muscles form. Daily habits are either helping or hurting your physique. A sloppy posture tends to make your stomach more relaxed, soft and mushy. Good posture goes hand-in-hand with a trim midsection. Practice good posture at all times, with the shoulders back and out, the chest and chin up and forward, and the waist tucked in tightly. Keep your back straight, and your shoulders balanced horizontally. Good posture enables you to maximize the appearance of your midsection; poor posture detracts from and hinders the appearance of your waist.

SUPPORTING EXERCISES

Training the waist is not an isolated event, as has been mentioned. In addition to working on the waist through exercises (such as those that have been presented), you have to diet correctly and perform aerobic work. In addition, the abdominals are not the only muscles you should pay attention to. In order to maximize your midsection muscularity, you need to work the opposite muscle group – the lower back. If any muscle group in the body becomes overdeveloped in proportion to the corresponding (opposite and balancing) muscle group, there is danger of injury to either of the two groups. For the waist, the lower back needs to be trained to prevent problems. And the opposite is true also. A strong waist helps prevent lower-back injuries.

What are some good lower-back exercises? There are three prominent exercises that will develop this region properly. They are good mornings, hyperextensions, and stiff-leg deadlifts. The good-morning exercise is performed by placing a light barbell across your upper back/shoulder region, then bending forward until your back is almost parallel with the floor. Repeat this 10 to 15 times to warm up the lower back. In the beginning of your training, perform this exercise without any weight. After you have several sessions under your belt you can use a light weight.

Achim Albrecht, Paul Dillett and Chris Cormier

Good posture enables you to maximize the appearance of your waist.

A hard muscular waistline can be more than a dream if you follow the *Six-Pack Abs* training program.
— Paul Dillett

The hyperextension is performed on the hyperextension unit, which is a padded steel structure found in most gyms. You can also perform this exercise off the ledge of any structure that gives you enough room to lower your upper body, provided your feet are supported (braced and immobile). You start from a prone position (with your lower body supported and stationary on the unit or ledge) and lower your upper body (it looks like a hanging reverse situp) to the floor. Then raise your upper body back to a flat position. The lower back and the buttocks do most of the work during this exercise, therefore, a regular workout including hyperextensions really benefits the lower-back region.

The stiff-leg deadlift is another great exercise for building the lower back. Slowly lift a fairly light barbell from the floor to your waist region, keeping the legs, back and arms as straight as possible, with your head up and looking forward. As you become accustomed to the exercise you can work with some heavier iron. Good form is very important. The deadlift will build a strong lower and upper back for your body.

You can choose any or all of these exercises to build your lower-back region so that it is a strong compliment to your abdominal region. At the minimum, perform a couple of sets of higher repetitions (10 to 20) for each exercise. It does not necessarily need to take much time to get in a few sets and the benefits are well worth the time spent. A strong stomach and lower back creates a protective band of muscles around your midsection that looks fantastic.

THE WORKOUT GUIDELINES

The following groups of waist exercises are divided into six workouts, each one gradually increasing the challenge to your muscles. The set and repetition range will also increase (positive incremental training adjustment) so that your waist region will be given sufficient challenge to continue to improve. If you have an easy time with the workout, move up to a more difficult workout, or perform the workout twice a day instead of once a day. The programs suggested are guidelines; they are not set in stone. No one is built the same. People have different bone structures, muscle development, etc., in addition to being different ages and having different genetic make-ups. Some people are more motivated than others. Adjustments are necessary to any training routine, and that holds true for the Six-Pack Abs training course. Feel free to add or delete exercises as necessary; however, try to follow the general guidelines of the workouts to ensure that you are building six-pack abs.

CONSISTENCY CONQUERS

Your waist will become accustom to the training after a period of time. You must push yourself in order to get to the next level. The training will be somewhat more difficult as you progress, but the results will be more pronounced – results you can see and that others will comment on. Consistent improvement is the best way to master the midsection. You don't have to be a superstar – just be consistent. Consistency plus a good hard workout will equal a great waist.

Shawn Ray and Pavol Jablonicky

SIX-PACK ABS TRAINING PROGRAM

Workout 1

Exercises	Sets	Repetitions
Partial Situps	2	30, 20
Crunches	2	15, 12
Bike Crunches	1	10

Workout 1 is fairly light. It is designed for those who have not trained the waist before, or who have not trained the waist for quite some time. It is important to perform all of the exercises in strict style and good form so as to build good habits for future waist workouts. Rest for a brief period of time between each exercise. Perform this waist workout 4 to 6 days a week for 1 to 2 weeks. If you have been performing some waist work recently you may want to use this routine for a week before moving onto workout 2 or skip workout 1 completely.

Workout 2

Exercises	Sets	Repetitions
Partial Situps	3	50, 30, 20
Crunches	2	20, 20
Bike Crunches	2	12, 10
V-Raises	2	10
Abdominal Vacuums	2	8

A strong waist helps prevent lower-back injuries.

The training level has escalated from the previous workout as the repetition ranges and some set ranges have been raised. Three more exercises have been included. If you cannot meet the repetition range, do the best you can. The idea is to increase your count each workout. If you can perform 35 repetitions of the partial situp, shoot for 40 repetitions in your next workout. It is best to reach the repetition goals through a series of "steps" or small incremental increases instead of trying to go all the way in one shot. Perform this workout 4 to 6 days per week for 1 to 2 weeks.

Extra Effort Tips: Extra effort tips will assist you in reaching an awesome abdominal section sooner. For the first extra effort tip, begin to perform "tummy tucks" throughout the day, when seated, standing, and even when walking.

Workout 3		
Exercises	**Sets**	**Repetitions**
Partial Situps	1	100
Crunches	3	30, 35, 20
Bike Crunches	2	15, 12
V-Raises	2	15
Leg Rolls	2	12
Abdominal Vacuums	3	10

Workout 3 increases the number of partial situps performed. You will go all out, attempting 100 repetitions in a nonstop fashion. Don't worry if you don't quite get there – just try to increase the repetition count each workout. Remember, there are several workouts per week. For instance, if you only perform 60 partial situps on Monday, try to reach 90 nonstop partial situps by Saturday. By taking the workout in bite-sized chunks, instead of trying to do it all at once, you will gradually build up your body to the level where it can handle the challenge. This workout also begins to include some exercise for the lower abdominals – the leg roll. Perform this workout 4 to 6 days per week for 1-1/2 to 2 weeks.

Extra Effort Tip: Perform the abdominal vacuum twice a day for quicker results.

Achim Albrecht and Thierry Pastel

Workout 4		
Exercises	**Sets**	**Repetitions**
Partial Situps	1	100
Crunches	2	35, 30
Bike Crunches	2	20, 15
V-Raises	2	20
Leg-Raise Crunches	2	12
Leg Rolls	2	15
Abdominal Vacuums	3	10

Start each workout with 100 repetitions of the partial situp. This will really hit the midsection hard. It would be more difficult to do all 100 repetitions at the end of the workout. If completing the full workout (all seven exercises) is too tough or time consuming, break the workout into two sessions – one in the morning, and one in the evening. Again, if you are not reaching the listed repetition ranges, keep striving to increase your daily repetition count. Compete with yourself, not the listed repetition range which is merely a guideline. Perform this workout 4 to 6 days per week for 1-1/2 to 2 weeks.

Extra Effort Tip: For quicker results, perform the full workout twice a day on a couple of days during the week.

Nasser El Sonbaty shows off his world-class physique alongside Vince Taylor, Roland Cziurlok and Chris Cormier.

Workout 5		
Exercises	Sets	Repetitions
Partial Situps	1	100
Crunches	2	40, 35
Bike Crunches	2	30, 20
V-Raises	3	25
Leg-Raise Crunches	2	20
Leg Rolls	3	18
Abdominal Vacuums	3	12

Consistency plus a good hard workout will equal a great waist.

The repetition range has increased for workout 5, and so has the set amount for some of the exercises. As mentioned earlier, if you are not making it through the workout, split it up into two sessions, one in the morning and one in the evening. Also, if you can't make the suggested repetition range, continue striving for improvement on your personal-best repetition efforts for each exercise. The reverse is also true; if you find the repetition ranges too low, shoot for a repetition range that is above the listed guidelines. Use this workout 4 to 6 days per week for 1-1/2 to 2 weeks.

Rory Leidelmeyer

Extra Effort Tip: *Start to work on the obliques with some side bends and side crunches. Perform a couple sets of each for 40 repetitions of side bends and 10 repetitions of the side crunch.*

Workout 6		
Exercises	Sets	Repetitions
Partial Situps	1	100+
Crunches	2	50, 40
Bike Crunches	2	30, 30
V-Raises	3	25
Leg-Raise Crunches	2	25
Leg Rolls	3	20
Abdominal Vacuums	3	15

At this point your abdominal strength will have greatly increased to a point where you should be able to handle well over 100 partial situps non-stop. The repetition count for workout 6 is increased somewhat, but if you take a look at the routine for workout 1 and compare it with workout 6, you can see a vast difference. By this point there will also be an immense difference in the appearance and strength of your waist. Workout 6 should put you close to the end of 60 days of waist-training. Your waist should be looking super when compared to what it was when you started this program two months ago. Use workout 6 for the next 4 to 8 weeks in a consistent fashion (4 to 6 days per week, with at least one double workout per week), and watch the exercises cut gut-burning grooves into your midsection.

FREE STYLE

After you have used workout 6 for a month, feel free to experiment and add in any of the other exercises listed earlier (hanging leg raises, extended crunches, side crunches, leg raises, etc.). You can also substitute any of these in place of one of the other exercises. If you find that one exercise does not work well for you, simply remove it and find another one that works better. Try to maintain your midsection at an intensity level of workout 6 so that your waist will always look "hot." Train hard and consistent, and occasionally rotate the waist exercises that you use to prevent your body from becoming too familiar with any one group of exercises. Use some creativity to make your workouts interesting — variety is the spice of life, and also a key tool in preventing training boredom. You will begin to really know your body (especially the midsection) and how it responds so take some chances and find out what works well and what doesn't.

Vince Taylor

Also include the lower-back training (mentioned earlier in the chapter) in at least one workout per week (try to get in more if possible). Build a good balance of strength between both the front and back regions of your mid-torso. Don't forget to include work on the obliques as well as the central abdominal region.

It is up to you to make this training program work. You are the one who ultimately decides the fate of your midsection — through working out or sitting in front of the television. You will not build six-pack abs unless you get active.

MAINTENANCE

Once you have used the Six-Pack Abs training program for half a year, you can afford to back off on the amount of time you put in per week and still maintain a great-looking midsection. If you are pleased with your progress after half a year, cut your workouts back to three times a week. Give yourself a rest day between workouts. Once you have built your body to a certain level it is possible to maintain it with less work than it took to get there. Take advantage of this principle and continue to work on your waist. Keep up the every-other-day routine even while you are traveling. The consistency will pay off as your stomach will always look superb. That is the goal of the awesome Six-Pack Abs training program — a hard and wicked waist.

REFERENCES

1. Vince Gironda and Robert Kennedy, Unleashing the Wild Physique (New York: Sterling Publishing, 1984), 107.
2. Gironda, Wild Physique, 107.
3. Gironda, Wild Physique, 106.

Milos Sarcev

Aerobic conditioning plays an important role in decreasing bodyfat stores to produce a tight, eye-catching midsection.
– Lee Apperson

CHAPTER THREE Burning Off Bodyfat

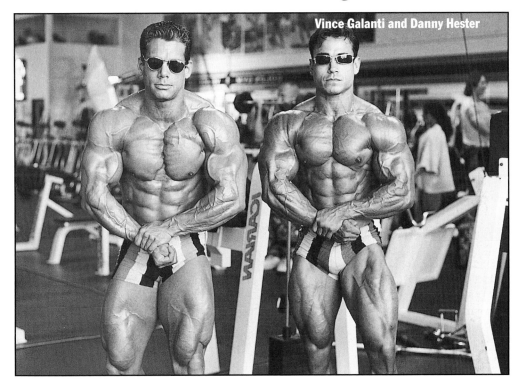

Vince Galanti and Danny Hester

Whipping the waist into shape is quickly and effectively accomplished through a triple-pronged attack. As mentioned earlier, the three elements of mastering the midsection are the actual waist-training exercises, diet, and aerobic conditioning. Some people make the mistake of getting stuck on one of these three areas, but to get total midsection development you must give attention to all three areas. Chapter one focused on exercises that stimulate the stomach muscles. Chapter four will focus on nutrition and diet. This chapter's primary focus is on aerobic conditioning – the element that burns fat. The exercises mentioned in the last chapter make your stomach muscular. Your diet prevents fat from accumulating, while aerobic conditioning takes off any fat that does happen to build up on your body. Each element plays a vital role in shaping and sculpting your stomach into a "hot" item.

THE AEROBIC CONCEPT

There are a lot of misconceptions floating around about aerobic conditioning. Some people don't use any aerobic exercises; others use a great deal. Some people go all out with superintensity; others use a low-key approach. What is the best approach concerning the aerobic concept of training?

Waler Andzei, PhD, notes that:

Activities that develop increased oxygen transportation and utilization are referred to as aerobic exercises. The word "aerobic" means "with oxygen" and indicates that the energy produced to do the work uses an oxygen system. By increasing your aerobic capacity, you can have a more efficient body, which translates into better training. Aerobic exercises produce a positive training effect on many parts of the body, such as the heart, lungs and muscles and the circulatory and endocrine systems. As a result, the body improves its ability to take in oxygen, transport the oxygen to where it's needed and then use the oxygen to produce energy for a workout. Aerobic exercise is also beneficial for preventing cardiovascular disease . . . you need to become acquainted with the overload principal . . . the overload works the same way in aerobics as it does in weightlifting: In order to improve your heart, lung and muscle function, you must subject your cardio-respiratory system to loads that are greater than what it's been accustomed to. This overload causes the system to adjust and increase its capacity to perform physical work. Because specific body systems require specific overloads, however, an overload for the cardiorespiratory system is different from what it would take to make strength gains or flexibility increases. You use four variables to produce and control the overload in aerobic training: intensity, duration, frequency, and mode of activity. Intensity is the workout's degree of difficulty, duration is the length, frequency is the number of training sessions per week, and mode refers to the specific activity.[1]

Joe DeAngelis

> ## The best training for burning fat is a moderate pace, and continuous activity that puts your heart rate "in the zone."

Aerobic exercises are exercises performed in a nonstop fashion for at least 15 to 20 minutes. It takes about this long for the fat-burning effect to occur. The initial blast of energy in any activity comes from glycogen, the fuel from carbohydrates. After about 15 to 20 minutes, the fuel source switches to fat. This means you need to work out in a nonstop fashion for at least 20 minutes.

Natural physique champion Peter Neilsen points out that:

Aerobic exercise serves three purposes in a health-maintenance program. The first goal is to increase HDL cholesterol (the beneficial kind), which aids in the prevention of cardiovascular disease. Second, aerobic exercise serves to maintain cardiovascular fitness levels – it strenghtens the heart and lungs. Third, it can be utilized to decrease bodyfat deposits by increasing the basal metabolic rate and burning bodyfat stores as a fuel source. To accomplish these objectives, aerobic exercises should be performed in a strict, training-specific manner.[2]

Nielsen goes on to point out that it is necessary to train at 70 to 80 percent of maximum heart rate (MHR) for your age to ensure benefits to the heart and lungs. However, he also notes that in order to lose bodyfat, the intensity of the training should be decreased to 55 to 65 percent of MHR. When you train with a continuous activity at this level your maximum heart rate will be "in the zone" that burns bodyfat. This "zone" is also echoed by Dr. Christine Lydon, who writes that "for minimum muscle burning and maximum fat burning, you should work out at 65 percent of your target heart rate."[3] She also makes another important point – if you train too hard for too long you face the problem of burning up muscle tissue. This is detrimental to your overall training, and can also smooth out your waist instead of sharpening it. That is the exact opposite of what you want. The best training for burning fat is a moderate pace, and continuous activity that puts your heart rate "in the zone."

Milos Sarcev

HEART-RATE TABLE

Age	MHR	55 %	65 %
20	200	112	130
25	195	107	127
30	190	105	123
35	185	102	120
40	180	99	117
45	175	96	114
50	170	94	110
55	165	91	107
60	160	88	104
65	155	85	101
70	150	83	97
75	145	80	94

Jean-Pierre Fux

If your age falls between or beyond the listed table, simply calculate the maximal rate by subtracting your age from 220. Multiply this number by 55 percent and 65 percent to calculate your bodyfat-burning range. How do you find your heart rate? Place a couple of fingers over the throbbing area in your neck (carotid artery) and count the beats per minute, or per 10 seconds (and multiply by 6 to get the one-minute rate). You can also find your pulse rate by checking the pulse of your wrist. Check your pulse rate throughout your workout to determine if you need to adjust the intensity to reach your target exercise range. Remember, to stay in the bodyfat-burning range since your goal is a trim midsection.

MUSCULAR REVELATION

The primary goal of the aerobic section of the Six-Pack Abs training course is to burn off bodyfat. A lot of people have a muscular midsection but unfortunately also have fat covering those muscles. You can perform thousands of waist exercises but to no avail if you carry an extra couple of inches of fat. Vince Gironda wrote that "the abdominal muscles are perhaps the most misunderstood area of all. Contrary to popular opinion, you cannot produce localized spot reduction by performing a few sets of situps every day. Only nutritional dieting and high-activity training with minimum rest periods will cause weight loss. Heart and lung action are very important to emulsify fat."[4]

As mentioned earlier, the best way to burn off bodyfat is to keep your heart rate "in the zone" for at least 20 minutes. Many people climb several flights of stairs or run a quick mile and then mentally pat themselves on the back and figure that they have taken care of their aerobic workout for the day. Actually, they haven't come near burning off any fat. Peter Neilsen writes that "to facilitate the loss of bodyfat, your exercise program must be geared differently. The body uses blood sugar and stored sugar in the form of glycogen in the skeletal muscles and liver as fuel for the first 20 minutes of activity. After that, the body switches to bodyfat stores as the preferred fuel source."[5] If a person runs a quick mile or two (perhaps at a six-minute mile rate), he or she would be using glycogen as fuel, and would not be touching bodyfat stores. In fact, a person running three miles at six miles per hour would still be using glycogen for fuel instead of bodyfat. The same is true for climbing a few sets of stairs. There is some muscular benefit, but no real fat-loss action. The manner in which you train is very important if you want to strip off bodyfat to reveal the muscles that lie underneath. Remember, specific waist-training activity builds the stomach muscles; aerobic exercises burn off the bodyfat. There will be no muscles to reveal if you do not perform direct waist exercises as given in chapter two; and there will be no way to see those muscles unless you get rid of bodyfat as noted in this chapter.

Jay Cutler

THE EXERCISES

There are a variety of good aerobic exercises that can be performed to burn off bodyfat. The key is to perform each exercise nonstop at a moderately quick pace (55 to 65 percent of maximum heart rate) for at least 20 minutes. You can use whatever type of exercise you want as long as it meets that criteria. Going beyond 20 minutes is even better for aerobic training. Studies have shown that exercises that last 60 to 90 minutes continue to burn off fat calories long after you have stopped exercising. An ideal aerobic workout is 45 to 60 minutes in length, but you can still gain benefit from a 20-minute workout.

Several of the more common aerobic exercises are described and presented in the Six-Pack Abs training program. However, if you have an exercise that works well for you and it is not listed here, go ahead and use it – for at least 20 minutes of nonstop activity that puts your heart rate at around 55 to 65 percent of your maximum heart rate.

FREQUENCY

The frequency for aerobic workouts should be three to five workouts per week. If you can only get in two workouts per week, do so, but realize it is not ideal for burning off fat. However, a few workouts are better than no workouts. The Six-Pack Abs routine will list several exercises, then provide a guideline for their use and frequency. Aerobic exercises can be mixed. In fact, it is probably better to mix different types of aerobic exercises to get a cross-training effect. Training with only one type of exercise all of the time can lead to training boredom. A variety of training types ensures maximum training interest. Flexibility is another important ingredient for a good workout mix. You may not always be able to perform a planned exercise due to the weather or a traveling schedule. That is why it is beneficial to have a variety of exercises to choose from.

COST

The training program for the aerobic section of the Six-Pack Abs routine does not necessarily have to cost anything at all. Exercises such as power walking, jogging, jumping rope, and stair stepping and many other great exercises can all be done at little or no cost. Of course, if you want, you can join a gym or club, but buying a gym membership is by no means a necessity to achieving maximum physique benefits. Low-cost training does not mean low-cost results – some of the best exercises are very basic in nature.

John Simmonds

GETTING STARTED

It is never a good idea to rush into a training program. Start off slow, and work up to a higher level of fitness. Just as with the direct waist workouts, it is best to gradually build up your muscle level of tolerance to the exercises. This principle also holds true for your lungs and heart. They gradually adapt to the stimulation that you present to them to meet the increased demands. Increasing a little at a time is the best way to work up to a higher level of fitness. Of course, if you are 35 or older and have not been involved in a regular fitness program for some time it is always wise to have your physician give you a green light before you start training.

Use an incremental approach to your aerobic training. For instance, if you can only go for 10 minutes nonstop in your first workout, then shoot for 12 minutes the next time, and 15 minutes in the third workout. The 20-minute aerobic training level is the minimum level to aim for once you have become accustomed to working out. Don't try to reach the 20-minute mark on the first workout if it is too difficult for your body. Once you have a few workouts under your belt you can make 20 minutes the minimum level. Don't stop there. If you can get in 45 to 60 minutes, do so. It will make your goal of six-pack abs occur all that much sooner.

Jog your way to a trimmer midsection.

JOGGING

Jogging is one of the better exercises for reducing bodyfat. Jogging can be performed at a moderate pace which is conducive to burning off bodyfat. One drawback to jogging too often is lower-body injury. The best way to incorporate jogging into your training schedule is to start off slowly, working up to a more brisk pace for several minutes, then slow down for a few minutes. Jogging should be used at least once a week, if possible.

STATIONARY BIKE

The stationary bike is an excellent tool to reduce bodyfat stores. The tempo of the workout can be controlled at just the pace you want. It also puts little stress on your lower body (it is a low-impact exercise as opposed to a high-impact exercise such as jogging). Most stationary bikes come equipped with a timer and a speed gauge which allows you to be precise in your workout intensity and duration. This is also a good exercise for those nasty winters when it is tough to get outside.

Only nutritional dieting and high-activity training with minimum rest periods will cause weight loss.

BIKE

Bike riding is another excellent manner in which to trim the body. As with the stationary bike, a bike ride puts very little stress on the lower-body structure. You can get in a good steady workout, burning lots of fat with the constant action of pumping thighs as you motor your body around town or on a bike path. This is an especially good exercise for the spring and summer months.

POWER WALKING

Power walking is probably the best exercise of all for burning off bodyfat. The pace is just about perfect and quite conducive to the body's fat-burning system. A power walk is a walk that is performed at a brisk pace, much like a march. If you can motor around at 3 to 4-1/2 miles per hour you will be right on target for burning bodyfat. You can test your pace by finding out how long it takes you to cover a mile, then divide that number into 60 (to account for 60 minutes in an hour). If you can cover a mile in 15 minutes, divide 60 minutes by 15. This equals a pace of 4 miles per hour, a great pace for using fat as fuel. Power walking is a low-impact exercise because the heavy pounding in running and jumping exercises does not occur. This keeps the lower body free from injury and able to train longer. Power walking can be performed almost anywhere. Hiking paths work well, as do local school tracks. Power walking can also be performed on a treadmill. An especially good workout is a treadmill set at an incline, which causes more calories to be burned during the duration of the workout. Because power walking is less intense than running you should aim for longer training sessions. Power walking should be one of the main exercises incorporated into the Six-Pack Abs workout.

A few workouts are better than no workouts.

Lee Apperson

SWIMMING

Swimming is another good exercise for burning off bodyfat. Swimming is a low-impact exercise. One drawback is that not everyone has access to a pool. If you do, take advantage of this exercise.

STAIR STEPPING/CLIMBING

A fantastic exercise for burning off bodyfat without cutting into the size of the muscles is stair climbing. This can be performed on a stair-stepping machine, or can be done on a staircase. Nonstop action is the key, and a steady pace should be used. This exercise will build and shape the legs as well as burn off unwanted bodyfat. If you use a stair-stepping machine be careful not to exceed your target fat-burning range (55 to 65 percent of maximum heart rate) as you can overdo the intensity level due to the variables on the machine. If you do not have access

Lee Apperson

Training with only one type of exercise all of the time can lead to training boredom. A variety of activities ensures maximum training interest.

to a staircase or a stair-stepping machine, simply build your own low-level step with a few pieces of wood. There is no need to spend a couple hundred bucks on a fancy little piece of plastic when you can build your own for under $10. The stair-stepper is an excellent exercise for burning bodyfat and ranks close to power walking as one of the very best. Take advantage of this exercise.

JUMPING ROPE

Jumping rope can burn off bodyfat. It is important to not get going too fast and to not jump on a solid surface like concrete. If you do jump on concrete you risk the possibility of developing shin splints and finding your aerobic-exercise schedule coming to a screeching halt. Use a surface that has been covered with rubber or carpet, or jump on low-cut grass. Jumping rope will give you a good workout and keep your training varied.

ROWING

A rowing machine can provide excellent fat-burning stimulation if it is performed at the right pace. Since you control the pace, you can take the time to check your pulse to find out if you are in the fat-burning zone. Alter your rowing pace to keep yourself in this zone to ensure that you are burning fat instead of glycogen or muscle.

AEROBICS

In addition to being the terminology for exercises that require a sustained uptake of oxygen, aerobics is also the general terminology for a specific type of exercise. This type of exercise stresses constant movement in a variety of positions and angles. Some aerobics also include the use of tools, such as a stair stepper. Most of the aerobics currently used are low impact so there is little chance of getting injured.

You can go to a club to participate, or simply watch a show on TV and follow along. After several sessions you will get the general drift and can make up your own aerobic workout. Aerobics is an excellent fat-burning exercise to use on the road, when you are traveling and stuck in a motel with no access to

A victorious win for Vince Taylor, a man with a superb set of abdominals.

> Consistency is the cornerstone for making any fat-burning program work.

cardio equipment. Simply use an aerobics workout to burn those extra calories you put on for dinner the previous evening.

PUTTING IT TOGETHER

These are a few of the more popular exercises among the many choices available for aerobic conditioning. Remember, the key is not to go as fast or as far as you possibly can, but rather to burn off bodyfat. This comes from moderate-paced training in a nonstop mode. Any exercise that allows you to do this will work to burn off bodyfat. Consistency is the cornerstone for making any fat-burning program work. A lot of people start with a New Year's resolution to lose some weight around the waist, only to stop shortly into the year. A diligent and persistent attack on the stomach will force it to finally yield. Choose the aerobic exercises that work for you, and experiment with a new type now and then. You may find that the new exercise works better and is more suited to your style. It is very important to keep working out. Consistency will not only burn off bodyfat and make your midsection look better – it will also enhance your overall health.

Workout	# of Cardio Sessions	Time Goal	Duration
1	3 per week	20 minutes	1 to 2 weeks
2	3 to 4 per week	30 minutes	1 to 2 weeks
3	4 to 5 per week	30 to 40 minutes	1-1/2 to 2 weeks
4	4 to 5 per week	45 minutes	1-1/2 to 2 weeks
5	4 to 6 per week	45 to 60 minute	1-1/2 to 2 weeks
6	4 to 6 per week	45 to 60 minutes, one workout of 90 minutes	4 to 8 weeks

THE WORKOUTS

As mentioned earlier, these workouts are suggested guidelines, and can be altered to suit your particular needs. However, try to stay as close as possible to the guidelines. These exercises should be used in conjunction with the waist workouts from chapter two. Perform both during the same week (although not necessarily on the same day).

Alq
Gurley

As you may have noticed, there is no direction concerning which of the aerobic exercises to use. You get to choose what you want to do as long as it meets the criteria set forth in the chapter. Match these workouts with the corresponding waist-training workouts to put together the full training schedule for the abdominals. For example, if you are on workout 3 for your direct waist-training, you should also be on workout 3 of the aerobic training.

The dual combination of a direct waist workout along with consistent aerobic conditioning will sculpt your stomach into a piece of art. There is one other element that will make this occur even quicker – a nutritious diet. The next chapter takes a look at this third element and how it can help you achieve six-pack abs.

REFERENCES

1. Walter D. Andzel, "Cardiorespiratory-endurance training," *Ironman* (October 1994), 150.
2. Peter Nielsen, "Slow Down!" *Natural Body Building & Fitness* (February 1995), 16.
3. "Christine Lydon: This Competitive Bodybuilder is Also a Kickboxer and Medical Doctor," *Martial Arts Training* (November 1995), 16.
4. Vince Gironda and Robert Kennedy, *Unleashing the Wild Physique* (New York: Sterling Publishing 1984), 107.
5. Nielsen, "Slow Down!" 16.

Lee Apperson and Debbie Kruck

CHAPTER FOUR

Diet and Nutrition

E veryone has a diet – the question is whether or not that diet is nutritious. Another question about an individual's diet is whether or not it is excessive, and looking at the population at large, it proabably is. The reason stems from the fact that the American diet has changed in a negative manner. The overweight population in America grew from 26 percent in the 1976 to1980 period to 34 percent in the 1988 to1991 period as reported in the Journal of the American Medical Association.[1] In 1860, fat contributed to 25 percent of the calories consumed. Today this figure has reached 39 percent.[2] Eating too much food, particularly fat or sweet food, creates problems within the body. The problems are compounded when you realize that fat is being stored over the area that you want to focus on, the waist. The body does distribute fat over the entire body, but most of it is stored around the waist. This obscures the waist muscles. Put simply, it looks gross. A fat midsection is very unappealing.

You have to be especially watchful of the waist as you grow older. You will often see physique champions who still look pretty good everywhere except their waist. Their back is big and strong, the chest firm, the legs and arms strong – but the waist has a large bulge. The waist is the weak link for most people, and becomes a bigger problem as they age. Since it is in the middle of the body it is virtually impossible to hide – it gets a lot of attention. The waist can be the most beautiful or the most unappealing body feature, depending upon how it is handled. Two of the three ways of mastering the waist have already been mentioned: Working the muscles of the waist with direct exercise, and burning off bodyfat with sustained aerobic exercise. The third piece of the physique sculpting puzzle is diet. The diet plays a major role in the way the body responds, reacts, and appears. Diet is a very important element that cannot be ignored. One doctor pointed out that "diet is extremely important. To stay

It is very likely that you will have to change some of your eating habits in order to maximize your physical potential.

The waist can be the most beautiful or the most unappealing body feature, depending on how it is handled.

lean and feel good, your workout is the most important thing you can do, but diet is not too far behind. If you don't eat right, it won't matter how hard you work out. If you don't eat right, you're going to have fat over your muscles, and you won't look the way you should. Fat is useless tissue. It is metabolically inactive, it does not contribute to strength, it stores toxins, and it is ugly."[3] That should be an incentive to get rid of fat. One of the best ways to prevent the buildup of fat is through diet. The diet can be utilized in two manners – to get rid of fat that is already on the body, and to prevent the accumulation of fat in the future.

Rich Gaspari

As the doctor mentioned in the previous paragraph, fat covers the muscles and prevents you from looking your best. It is bad enough when the muscle groups such as the biceps or chest are covered by a layer of fat, but when it is the waist it seems even more unappealing. The body does not deposit most of its fat on the arms or chest – it sinks to the waist (and for women it also seems to accumulate in the hip/thigh region). So if you want to sculpt a super "hot" stomach, to fashion that great "jewel" appearance in the midsection, you have to get rid of the fat that is there and prevent any future fat from building up. This is best achieved through your diet. One fitness guru contends that diet plays an 85 percent role in shaping the physique. Others say that diet makes up at least 50 percent of the necessary effort to shape the body. In the Six-Pack Abs training course, diet is one of the three elements, but that does not mean it only plays one-third the role. To correctly balance the three components of Six-Pack Abs training, the importance of each would be 40 percent diet, 40 percent aerobic exercise, and 20 percent direct waist workouts. As you can see, diet is a very important factor when it comes to mastering your midsection.

CHANGE

It is very likely that you will have to change some of your eating habits in order to maximize your physical potential. But you have to pay a price if you want to look good. If a hot body could be achieved without any real effort, everyone would have a great physique and then having a great physique would be no big deal. However, since it is tough to build an awesome body, it carries more honor and respect when you do achieve that goal. You have to pay a price. It is said that nothing in life is free, and neither is an attractive physique. Part of that price is a more disciplined approach to your diet.

This all sounds difficult, but there is some good news. A tighter diet does not necessarily mean that you are reduced to an intake of lettuce and dry bread.

A diet can be fashioned to be very nutritious as well as tasty. There has been a tremendous shift in the food industry in the past decade and now you can "have your cake and eat it too," so to speak. There are products that give you the necessary nutrition and are also delicious. You can get nonfat or low-fat cookies, pudding, potato chips, pizza, salad dressings, sour cream, yogurt, and a host of other desirable foods that have had the fat content removed or reduced. Many eating establishments now offer a line of low-fat foods so that you don't have to blow your diet when dining out. Dieting is now easier than it has ever been. Also, many of the traditional foods in a diet can be spiced up with nonfat additives to make them taste good – for instance, a baked potato can be topped with nonfat sour cream or nonfat salad dressing for a great-tasting meal.

THE BAD GUYS – SUGAR AND FAT

There are two main items to avoid in any good diet – sugar and fat. Refined sugar and fat are the cause of most problems for people's physiques. A little bit of either is not a problem, but most people eat an excessive amount of both. Many foods contain either or both of these "bad guys." One of the main maneuvers in the Six-Pack Abs training course is to remove as much refined sugar and fat from the diet as possible. By doing so the body will strip away the unwanted inches around the waist and reveal the muscularity beneath.

THE BASIC ELEMENTS

There are several basic elements in nutrition which comprise the total food picture. Having a basic knowledge of these elements and how they interact in the body is very helpful to putting together a sound diet. An overview of these elements will be provided to give you a general grasp of their function in your physique.

Diet is a very important factor when it comes to mastering your midsection.

PROTEIN

The most crucial substance of all (after water, of course) is protein. In French the word protein is spelled proteine which means "primary substance to the body." This was derived from the late Greek work proteios which means "primary." That word came from an earlier work, protos, which means "first." The first and therefore most primary element in nutrition is protein.

The dictionary defines protein as "any of a group of complex nitrogenous organic compounds of high molecular weight that contains amino acids as their basic structural units and that occur in all living matter and are essential for the growth and repair of animal tissue." That all sounds fancy, but the essence of the statement is wrapped up in the final part of the sentence which says that protein is "essential for growth and repair." Protein is the most vital food element in any diet. Christine Lydon, MD, notes that if you get an adequate intake of protein:

1. Your muscles will appear harder and fuller.
2. You will feel stronger.
3. You will notice decreased muscle soreness.
4. You will be more rested after the same recovery time.
5. You will probably observe a decrease in bodyfat.
6. You will have an increase in lean muscle mass.[4]

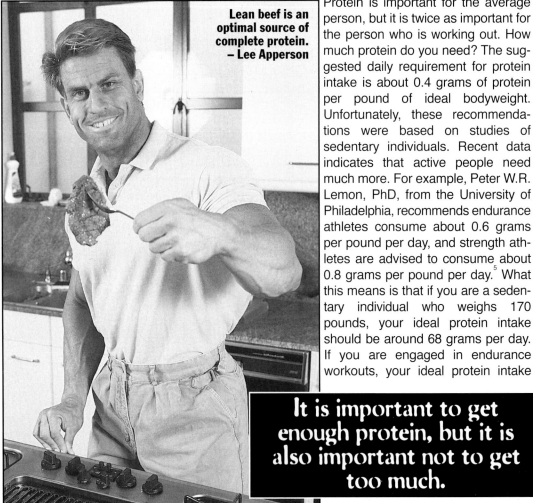

Lean beef is an optimal source of complete protein.
– Lee Apperson

Protein is important for the average person, but it is twice as important for the person who is working out. How much protein do you need? The suggested daily requirement for protein intake is about 0.4 grams of protein per pound of ideal bodyweight. Unfortunately, these recommendations were based on studies of sedentary individuals. Recent data indicates that active people need much more. For example, Peter W.R. Lemon, PhD, from the University of Philadelphia, recommends endurance athletes consume about 0.6 grams per pound per day, and strength athletes are advised to consume about 0.8 grams per pound per day.[5] What this means is that if you are a sedentary individual who weighs 170 pounds, your ideal protein intake should be around 68 grams per day. If you are engaged in endurance workouts, your ideal protein intake

It is important to get enough protein, but it is also important not to get too much.

Excessive intake of refined sugar and fats should be avoided. Substitute natural foods for the unhealthy "goodies."

would be 102 grams. If you are engaged in strength-building activities your protein intake should be 136 grams per day.

You can find your ideal protein intake by using the following multiplier:		
Weight	**Activity Level**	**Ideal Protein Intake**
Your weight = _____ lb	sedentary = 0.4	weight x 0.4 = _____
Your weight = _____ lb	endurance = 0.6	weight x 0.6 = _____
Your weight = _____ lb	strength = 0.8	weight x 0.8 = _____
Your weight = _____ lb	mixed = 0.7	weight x 0.7 = _____

The mixed training level is probably best for the Six-Pack Abs workout since the training is a mix between endurance and strength. For example, if you weigh 200 pounds and are actively engaged in the Six-Pack Abs training program then you would multiply your bodyweight by 0.7 to find that your ideal protein intake is 140 grams per day. If you weigh 130 pounds, you would multiply 130 by 0.7 to find that your ideal protein intake is 91 grams per day. You can use this chart to find your exact protein requirements. Note the body's increased need for protein for those who workout. Protein is needed for repair and growth, two factors that come about when you train.

It is important not to exceed the amount of protein needed by your body. When you eat excess protein, the body stores it as fat. If you need 130 grams of protein and consume 160 grams, the extra 30 grams of protein will be stored as bodyfat (and most of it will probably be stored around your waist, frustrating your efforts to trim your midsection). It is important to get enough protein, but it is also important not to get too much. So pay attention to what you are eating. Read labels to find out how much protein is in each item of food you eat.

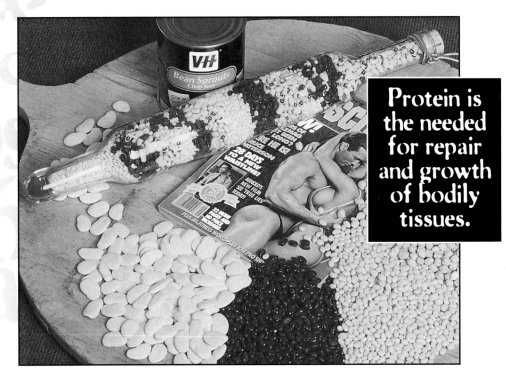

Protein is the needed for repair and growth of bodily tissues.

QUALITY PROTEIN

The quality of the protein that you eat is also very important. Quality is noted by the terms biological value (BV) and protein efficiency ratio (PER). The higher the number on the BV scale, the better the protein. Egg protein is listed as the highest, with a BV of 100. Fish comes in at anywhere from 75 to 90, and rice has a BV of 86, which is higher than most plant proteins. Corn has a BV of only 40. In general, a biological value of 70 or better indicates acceptable quality.[6]

The protein efficiency ratio indicates how well the body digests and uses protein. The higher the number the better the protein (generally anything in the 3.4 plus range is great). Some protein supplements will list the efficiency ratio on the side of the can or jug.

Meat and egg proteins are of a higher quality than vegetable proteins. This is because there are 22 amino acids of which eight are essential and plant sources do not contain all of the essential aminos. The eight essential amino acids are called essential because the body desperately needs them. Meat, dairy products, and eggs contain the essential amino acids. If you are eating vege-tables as a source of protein you will have to mix and match different types to receive the required aminos your body needs. It is better to get your protein from complete sources. These sources are eggs, fish, turkey breast, chicken breast, lean beef, skim milk and skim milk products (cheese, yogurt, etc.). It is also important to get your protein from sources that have little or no fat. That is why lean beef and skim milk are best.

CARBOHYDRATES

Carbohydrates are the fuel source for your workouts. Famous football coach Vince Lombardi drilled into his players that "the difference between success and failure is in energy." That is true for you, too. If you do not have enough energy to work out, your workouts and your training program will fail. Carbs provide you with the fuel you need for the intense workouts required to burn off fat.

Carbohydrates are short-term energy units as opposed to fats, which are long-term stored energy. Carbohydrates are the chief source of energy for all body functions and muscular exertion and are necessary to assist in the digestion and assimilation of other foods. Carbohydrates provide immediately available calories for energy by producing heat in the body when carbon in the system unites with oxygen in the bloodstream. Carbohydrates also help regulate protein and fat metabolism; fats require carbohydrates for their breakdown in the liver.[7] As you can see, carbohydrates are necessary for many functions in the body – one of which is assisting in the elimination of fat.

THREE CARBS

There are three types of carbohydrates – simple, complex (starches) and cellulose. Cellulose is a bulky, fiber type of material (fruit and vegetables skins, etc.) that is often indigestible and does not provide much energy. Cellulose is vital, though, because it provides bulk necessary for intestinal action and helps in elimination.[8] It should also be included in the diet because it creates a kind of thermogenetic effect (a fired-up metabolism) because the body has to crank up the heat as it works to eliminate the bulky fiber, which in turn burns more calories. In addition to this fat-reduction potential, fibrous carbohydrates can help prevent certain types of cancer.

Carbohydrates are the fuel source for your workouts.

Simple carbohydrates (sugars) are the quick-energy-release type of carbs. These simple sugars are found in fruit and honey and are very easily digested. Another type is the double sugar, such as table (refined) sugar which requires some digestive action. Simple carbohydrates are quickly digested compared to complex carbohydrates. The rapid transformation of simple sugars makes them great for a quick energy uptake or refuel, but large intake of sugar will cause the excess to be stored as bodyfat. Sugar, which has four calories per gram, gets into your system rapidly and increases your blood-sugar level. This is bad because it allows your fat cells to accept calories in the form of fat.[9] Complex carbohydrates are a better source for energy. One fitness author noted that:

Complex carbohydrates ordinarily are the ideal energy source. They are slowly digested and absorbed and their calories are burned in a prolonged, even way, which provides a steady release of the critical anabolic hormone insulin. Fiber-rich carbs ensure good elimination, too. The amount of carbs needed each day varies widely depending upon biochemical individuality and on training intensity and duration. All endurance athletes need far more carbohydrates than proteins. A runner can train with greater intensity for longer periods of time with full stores of muscle glycogen. Glucose from the blood and liver is less efficient. When you exercise hard, glycogen is your main fuel. Elite athletes show muscle-glycogen levels twice as high as sedentary persons. Regular exercise is the primary stimulus for topped-off glycogen storage. Almost immediately after exercise ends the enzyme necessary to refill glycogen stores increases in activity. If carbohydrate intake is plentiful during the next couple of hours, you recover quickly. Oddly enough, this is one time when simple rather than complex carbs may be preferred. The liver likes to be flooded with fructose such as is found in fruit juices and sports drinks. The muscles are ravenous and thirsty, so this is a perfect time to succumb to the seductive sucrose in soda. After the initial hydration and ingestion of simple carbs, consumption of a protein drink (milk or protein powder) can synergistically speed up the repacking of muscle glycogen. While carbohydrate calories are being spared for glycogen synthesis, lipids are vigorously oxidized after exercise almost as effectively as they were during training.[10]

For weight loss, muscle building and energy utilization consume 80 percent of your carbohydrates from complex sources such as potatoes, yams, pastas and beans.

So what does this mean? It means that for weight loss, muscle building and energy utilization, it is best to get your energy intake from complex carbohydrates except right after a workout, when it is better to refuel with simple sugars.

What are the best complex carbohydrates? The best sources of complex carbohydrates include rice, cereal grains, found in bread (natural, unrefined is much better than the processed white bread, etc.), potatoes, sweet potatoes, yams, pastas, cereals, and beans. Use these sources to get the fuel that you need for your workouts.

A good rule of thumb is to consume most of your carbohydrates (around 80 percent) from complex sources. Unfortunately, most people get 80 percent of their carbohydrates from simple sugars. If you switch this percentage your waistline will begin to look a lot better. Your body needs more complex carbohydrates and less simple sugars. Remember, too much simple sugar is undesirable because it causes a large and rapid insulin release, and insulin is a potent stimulus for fat storage.[11] Eat complex carbohydrates for most of your meals, and allow yourself some simple sugars, but generally right after a workout.

Hamdullah
Aykutlu

FAT

Fat is the big bad monster when it comes to the abdominals. Fat covers the abdominals with its lardy substance and obscures the muscles that lie underneath. Fat looks gross, and the more of it there is, the worse it looks; however, it is not all bad. Fat does carry several vital functions including the transportation of vitamins, and helps with brain functions. Fat is in essence a necessary evil, but anything beyond that small amount works in a negative fashion, especially if you are concerned about the appearance of your waist and your health.

The problem with fatty foods is that they taste good. Unfortunately, they are deadly, and take their tole on the body over years. For instance, fatter men are 2/5 times more likely to die of heart disease than lean men.[12] Fat is a slow killer. It also kills any chance you might have of a sharp midsection.

The key to fat intake is to consume a very small amount. A little fat goes a long way. This is true because fat has such a dense caloric value. Fat is super-high in calories. Fat contains 225 percent more calories per gram than either protein or carbohydrates. To make matters worse, fat accumulates on the body easily. Fat is also hidden in many menus – you get much more than you bargain for. Fast food and junk food are usually very high in fat. Fried foods are usually the worst culprits, so skip the donuts and french fries.

LOW INTAKE

The key to a better diet is to greatly reduce your intake of fat (and sugar). If you are like most people, this will probably mean a big change in your diet. The typical American diet gets almost 40 percent of its caloric contribution from fat.[13] Some nutritionists recommend that a diet receive no more than 20 percent of its calories from fat. This is where the recommendation for the Six-Pack Abs course starts, however, the diet becomes even more strict. This will allow for further fat reduction, enabling you to see your abdominal muscles.

Water is the most crucial element for the body to function.

The low-fat diet that corresponds with the individual workouts looks like this:

Workout	Fat intake (% of calories)	Sugar Intake
1	20 percent	cut in half
2	15 percent	cut in half again
3	15 percent	hold even
4	10 percent	hold even
5	10 percent	hold even
6	15 percent	hold even

Note that the reduction in fat is a reduction in total caloric value. How do you find out what your reduction should be? Read labels.

READING LABELS

Foods carry labels that tell how many grams of protein, carbohydrates, and fat are contained in that food. Labeling provides crucial information for determining how nutritious a food is.

To determine the percentage of calories each food nutrient provides you will have to do a little math. Each gram of protein or carbohydrtae contains four calories and each fat gram contains nine calories.

Check the label and: Multiply Protein by 4
Multiply Carbohydrates by 4
Multiply Fat by 9

Total the results and divide by the individual amounts to get the correct percentage of calories for each nutrient.

Example: If a bowl of stew has 14 grams of protein, 22 grams of carbohydrates and 7 grams of fat, you would make your calculations like this:

Protein	14	x	4 =	56	calories from protein
Carbohydrates	22	x	4 =	88	calories from carbohydrates
Fat	7	x	9 =	63	calories from fats
Total				207	calories

This food has a total of 207 calories. The 63 calories from the fat are divided into the total caloric count (207). This produces a 30-percent indicator which means that this food is too high in fat (it should be in the 10- to 20-percent range for the Six-Pack Abs diet). If the stew contained only 1 to 4 grams of fat, the stew would be acceptable. You can check any food in this manner. Make certain to keep your fat intake from a total of all foods in the range listed earlier to maximize fat-reduction.

You can also find out the amount of simple carbohydrates (sugars) as opposed to total carbohydrates in the same manner, by checking labels. Total all carbohydrates, simple and complex (complex is sometimes listed as "other") and then divide by the amount of complex carbohydrates.

Example: If a cereal product has 8 grams of simple carbohydrates and 33 grams of complex carbohydrates, you would multiply each by 4 and total the amount:

Simple carbohydrates	8 x 4 =	32 calories
Complex carbohydrates	33 x 4 =	132 calories
Total	=	164 calories

This food product gets over 80 percent of its caloric content from complex carbohydrates; therefore, it is a very good source of carbohydrates. Reading labels will assist you in sound dieting practices.

NATURAL

Eat as much of your food in as natural a state as possible. The more natural the food the better. Processing damages most foods by taking out the good stuff (fiber, vitamins and minerals, etc.) and adding in extra sugar, salt and other not-so-nutritious items. It is best to eat fruits and vegetables raw, skin and all, for the greatest nutritional effect on the body.

WATER

Water is the most crucial element for the body to function. You can go for quite a while without food, but not so with water. You will need to drink a lot of water to flush the fat out of your system in the Six-Pack Abs dieting approach. Some people mistakenly think that they should reduce water intake to get smaller. This is not true. Drinking more water will help you get smaller in the long run. Water is the most important nutrient for the body. Water is the primary transporter of nutrients and removes toxins from the body and helps flush out fat. Drink a lot of water. How much? When you are working out, you will need between 1 and 2 gallons a day. A sedentary person needs 0.5 to 1 gallon a day; on this program you will be

If you want to melt the extra inches off your midsection you have to submit to a more regulated diet, and that includes increasing your water intake.

quite active and need much more. Drink water that is clean and free of chlorine for best results.

VITAMINS AND MINERALS

A steady intake of vitamins and minerals is necessary for maintaining good health. A good inclusive one-a-day vitamin and mineral supplement should cover the bases for you. Make certain that you buy a vitamin and mineral supplement that contains 100 percent of the recommended daily allowance (RDA) for each vitamin and mineral. Make certain that the supplement contains chromium picolinate (a trace mineral that most American diets lack and which is necessary for proper insulin function) and 100 percent of the RDA for biotin, a B vitamin that is often not contained in a multisupplement. You don't need supermega doses of these vitamins and minerals – a one-a-day will be enough.

SMALL MEALS

For the best dietary results it is wise to eat several small meals a day as opposed to a few large ones. Several small meals will keep your metabolism active without overwhelming it. Pyramid your meals downward – eat more in the morning, and less in the evening.

SAMPLE DIET:

Breakfast	2 to 3 egg whites with one yolk, potato, toast, juice
Snack	bowl of low-fat cereal with fruit and nonfat milk
Lunch	turkey sandwich with nonfat dressing, vegetables, fruit for desert
Snack	nonfat yogurt, fruit, rice cake
Dinner	lean beef or chicken with pasta, vegetables, fruit for desert

There are literally hundreds of meal combinations you can make based on nutritious foods. Allow yourself a "junk" day every now and then to keep from having to drop the diet. If you give yourself the freedom to have a tasty snack once every few days then your diet won't seen so difficult. But make certain the "junk" snacks are few and far between.

DIET – THE DECIDING FACTOR

Your diet plays a big role in the Six-Pack Abs picture. If you want to maximize your midsection, it is crucial that you follow a tight diet. The diet is perhaps the most important element for whacking the fat off your waist. If you want to melt the extra inches off your midsection you have to submit to a more regulated diet. Use the guidelines in this chapter to put together a personal dieting program that will make you trim and tight.

Mike Ashley

It is best to eat fruits and vegetables raw, skin and all, for the greatest nutritional effects on the body

REFERENCES

1. "Hot Breaking Research," Muscular Development (December 1995), 22.
2. "Hidden Fat in the American Diet," Nutrition 21 (San Diego: n.p.1994), 1.
3. "Christine Lydon: This Competitive Bodybuilder is also a Kickboxer and Medical Doctor," Martial Arts Training (November 1995), 17.
4. Christine Lydon, "Six Great Reasons to Increase Your Protein Intake," Martial Arts Training (November 1995), 22.
5. Lydon, "Protein Intake," 22.
6. Eva May Hamilton and Eleanor Whitney, Nutrition: Concepts and Controversies (St. Paul: West Publishing Company 1979), 131.
7. John Kirschmann, Nutrition Almanac, 2nd ed. (New York: McGraw-Hill, 1984), 5.
8. Kirschmann, Almanac, 5.
9. Christine Lydon, "Protein Intake," 17.
10. Chris Rand, "Nutrition Knowledge, A Guide to Building a Better Body," Men's Workout (September 1994), 39.
11. John Parillo, "For Fruitful Dieting, Cut Out the Fruit!" Natural Physique and Fitness (February 1995), 53.
12. Susan McDaniel, "Muscle Media Index," Muscle Media 2000 (July 1995), 36.
13. "Hidden Fat in the American Diet," Nutrition 21 (San Diego: n.p.1994), 1.

Thierry Pastel

CHAPTER FIVE

The Total Training Package

A s you know by now, training the midsection is a multidimensional endeavor. You must work on three primary areas — direct abdominal-training, aerobic conditioning, and nutritious dieting. Each of these three areas must be given sufficient emphasis in order for total abdominal-training to occur. Neglect any of the three and you cause a short-circuit of the overall effect of the total midsection program. Yes, you can get some gains by focusing on only one or two of the areas, but the gains are only marginal when compared to what they could be if you used the full program. By working on all three elements you can reach your "super stomach" goals more rapidly and completely. There is a synergistic effect that occurs when you put all three areas together in your training program. The synergistic effect is such that the combination of the three elements produces an effect much better than any of the individual parts alone. This "team effort" drives the momentum of your training toward your goals.

MEASUREMENTS

Before you get started, before you even begin any direct waist work, before you take the first step in your aerobic program, or change your diet, you need to take your measurements. It is very important to find out what they are now, as well as when you finish (although you never really finish, you do need to check your progress in a visible and notable manner). It will also be encouraging to watch

Flavio Baccianini, David Dearth, Aaron Baker, Vince Taylor and Jim Quinn

the changes occurring around your mid-section. As your midsection becomes tighter and trimmer, so will the rest of your body. Measurements are great – they will provide concrete evidence that you have made real progress.

Take a picture of yourself (or have a friend take the picture) in a small swimsuit before you get started on this program. Save the picture for later reference. Measure your waist. Measure it at your belly button, and lower, by the hip area where you wear a belt. Note these measurements in a notebook, and put the date down also. Flex your stomach muscles in the mirror and note whether or not you can see any muscles. Weigh yourself. Also check your fat percentage. You can have this performed at a health clinic, or you can buy a caliper (they can be obtained through an ad in a fitness magazine; most cost around $20). Note your current bodyfat percentage.

Keep these measurements and the photo(s) for future reference. You can recheck them once you are a month into the *Six-Pack Abs* program. You will probably notice some very positive changes in your physique.

Lee Priest

Measurements are great – they provide concrete evidence that you have made real progress.

ACCOUNTABILITY

One of the best ways to ensure that you stay on course for reaching your waist-training goals is to have some accountability. You can do this in two ways. First, buy a notebook and write down your training goals. Check this from time to time to stay committed to the vision you have for an awesome waist. Second, get a friend involved. Find someone who also wants to knock some inches off his/her waist and become training partners. You don't necessarily have to train at the same time, (although you could) but you can keep track of each other and encourage each other to keep going to reach the goals you originally set out to obtain.

GOALS AND COMMITMENT

Your goals and your commitment to them are a very powerful force, working in your favor. Set some realistic goals (perhaps 2 to 3 inches off the waist, or being able to see your abdominal muscles when you contract and flex them) and then stay at it until you reach those goals. Take it one step at a time and remain consistent. If you happen to come to a stumbling block (like getting sick or having to abandon the program for some reason), get back up and start again until you get what you want – a "hot" waist. Remember, no one is going to build your body for you – it is your task alone. You have to diet and work out to achieve the physique you desire. But the reward is well worth it.

DOUBLE-CHECK

After all the tough stuff you get to have some fun. When you have been on the Six-Pack Abs routine for two months, haul out the picture that you took at the beginning of the program. Check the notebook where your initial measurements were. You will notice that you most likely look a lot better, and are quite a bit trimmer. Your measurements should have improved a great deal. Your waist should now look rugged instead of soft.

Go out and celebrate with a pizza, banana split, or chocolate cake, or however you want to celebrate your training improvement. The next day get back at the task of staying in shape. You won't need to work quite as hard to maintain your abdominals as you did when you started training. You can let your fat intake range from 10 to 20 percent instead of being superstrict all of the time. On occasion you can get away with a three-times-a-week aerobic workout instead of the regular four- to six-times-a-week schedule. You don't have to do quite as many crunches and other direct waist work to maintain your midsection as you did to develop your midsection initially. Monitor your progress; if you find a little fat accumulating or see that some of the muscularity has been slipping away, increase the involvement, intensity, or duration of each of the three elements until you have regained the ground you lost.

CYCLE

You can use the waist-training you have learned whenever and wherever you want. You can adjust it up or down to meet your specific needs. You may find that there are certain times when you want to look sharper, when you need that edge of an extrarugged waist. You can simply adjust the tempo of the three primary elements of abdominal-training to get the change you need. You might bring your daily caloric fat intake under 10 percent for a short period. You may increase your aerobic workouts from 40 minutes four times a week to 60 plus minutes six times a week. You may double up on your direct waist-training time. It is all up to you – you control the variables. Adjust the three elements until you get the look you want – six-pack abs!

Achim Albrecht, Chris Cormier and Thierry Pastel

Set some realistic goals that you want to achieve and then stay at it until you reach those goals.

Index

Contributing Photographers

Jim Amentler, Alex Ardenti, Garry Bartlett, Paula Crane, Ralph DeHaan Irvin Gelb, Robert Kennedy, Jason Mathas, Mitsuru Okabe